BIG MACHINES

Trucks

David and Penny Glover

FRANKLIN WATTS
LONDON•SYDNEY

This edition 2007

Franklin Watts
338 Euston Road, London, NW1 3BH

Franklin Watts Australia
Level 17/207 Kent Street, Sydney, NSW 2000

Copyright © Franklin Watts 2004

Series editor: Sarah Peutrill
Designer: Richard Langford
Art director: Jonathan Hair
Illustrator: Ian Thompson
Reading consultant: Margaret Perkins, Institute of Education, University of Reading
Picture credits: Harold Chapman/Topham: 19t. Corbis: 14. Duomo/Corbis: 23b. Martyn
Goddard/Corbis: 17. Darrell Gulin/Corbis: 10. Walter Hodges/Corbis: 12, 15t, 20, 21t. Lester
Lefkowitz/Corbis: 22. Photo Courtesy of Mack Trucks, Inc: 9b, 15b, 16t, 19b. Charles O'Rear/Corbis:
16b. Picturepoint/Topham: 11t, 18. Courtesy of Volvo Trucks Ltd: front cover, 4, 6, 7, 8, 9t, 11b, 13, 21b,
23c. Every attempt has been made to clear copyright. Should there be any inadvertent omission,
please apply to the publisher for rectification.
With particular thanks to Volvo Trucks Ltd and Mack Trucks, Inc for permission to use their photos.

A CIP catalogue record for this book is available from the British Library.

Dewey number: 629.224
ISBN: 978 0 7496 7806 7

Printed in Malaysia

Franklin Watts is a division of Hachette Children's Books, an Hachette Livre UK company.

Contents

On the move

Trucks are big transport machines. A truck's job is to carry heavy loads from one place to another.

Road trucks carry goods like food for us to eat. They are also called lorries.

BIG FACT

A big road truck weighs 40 tonnes. That's as much as five elephants!

Dumper trucks carry soil and rocks around building sites and quarries. Their giant wheels and strong bodies are made for rough work.

Tractor unit

The front part of the truck is called the tractor unit. This is where the driver sits in the cab.

Cab

Tractor unit

Engine

The truck's powerful engine is underneath the cab. It turns the wheels to pull the truck along. Truck engines use diesel fuel.

An articulated truck has a separate tractor and trailer. This means it can bend when it turns a corner.

Trailer

A rigid truck does not bend. The tractor and trailer are fixed together.

The trailer

The trailer carries the load. It does not have its own engine. Its wheels just turn around as the tractor pulls. Different trailers do different jobs.

Flatbed trailers are good for carrying awkward loads.

This truck's flatbed trailer is carrying a tractor.

A box trailer can be loaded with goods in packages.

This truck has a refrigerated box trailer to keep food fresh.

A dumper truck's trailer tips to dump its load.

Cylinder

Hydraulic ram

Piston

Hydraulic rams tip the trailer up. Oil pushes a piston out of a cylinder to make the lifting force.

The driver's cab

A truck driver spends many hours in the cab. The cab is high up so the driver has a good view. The seat is well sprung to even out bumps in the road.

Steering wheel   **Instrument panel**

Gear stick

The driver uses the steering wheel to drive the truck safely along the road.

Steering wheel

Lever

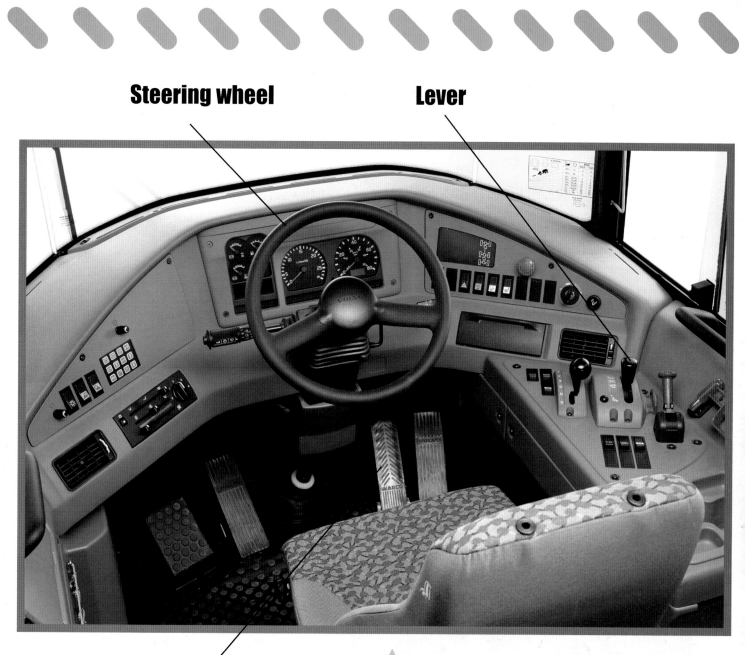

Foot pedals

▲ Foot pedals make the dumper truck go forwards and stop.

Dumper trucks have levers as well. These work the hydraulic rams that tip the trailer up and down.

Wheels and axles

Each wheel on a big truck is taller than a person. The thick rubber tyre grips the road.

Grooves

Grooves help to make the tyre grip on the road.

Wheel nuts hold the wheels on.

The wheels turn around axles. The axles are rods that fix the wheels to the truck's body.

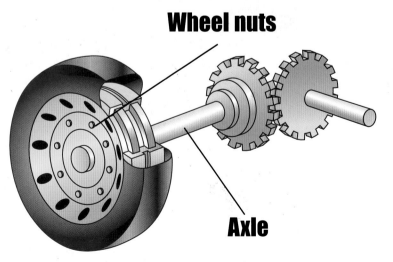

Wheel nuts

Axle

The grooves take water from under the wheel when it rains, so the truck does not skid.

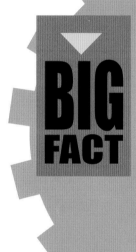

BIG FACT

A big truck has 10 or more wheels. Lots of wheels spread the truck's great weight so that it does not damage the road.

This truck has five wheels on each side.

Lights, mirrors and sounds

Before overtaking, the truck driver checks the wing mirrors. If there are no other vehicles coming, it is safe to pull out.

In the wing mirror the driver of this truck can see that the road behind is empty. ▶

At night the driver turns on the truck's lights. Powerful headlamps light up the road ahead.

Headlamp

Special loads

A car transporter carries cars.
It is a double-decker.

Top deck

Bottom deck

▲ This car transporter is
carrying eight old cars.

A road tanker carries liquid in its steel tank. Some tankers carry petrol to garages, others collect milk from farms.

This tanker is carrying petrol.

Drum

A cement mixer carries wet cement in its giant drum.

The drum turns as the truck drives to the building site - mixing the cement as it goes.

Truck driving

Driving a road truck is called trucking. It is a difficult job.

Truck drivers often have to drive hundreds of kilometres each day along busy roads.

Truck drivers must take plenty of breaks. Driving long distances is very tiring.

Truck drivers sometimes have to drive in bad weather like fog or snow.

Driving a dumper truck is a difficult job, too. Quarries and building sites are dangerous places.

Quarries have rough, high tracks, not proper roads.

Gigantic trucks

The biggest trucks of all
are giant dumper trucks.
They work in quarries
and mines.

BIG FACT

The Liebherr T282
is the world's
biggest truck. It
can carry a load
the weight of
50 elephants!

The wheels
on a giant
dumper truck
are twice as
tall as a man.

The longest trucks in the world are called road trains. They have more than one trailer and carry loads across Australia.

A big road train is long enough to reach from one side of a football ▼ field to the other.

In the sport of monster trucking, trucks with huge wheels drive over old cars.

Make it yourself

Make a model dumper truck.

You will need:

An adult to help

Paints

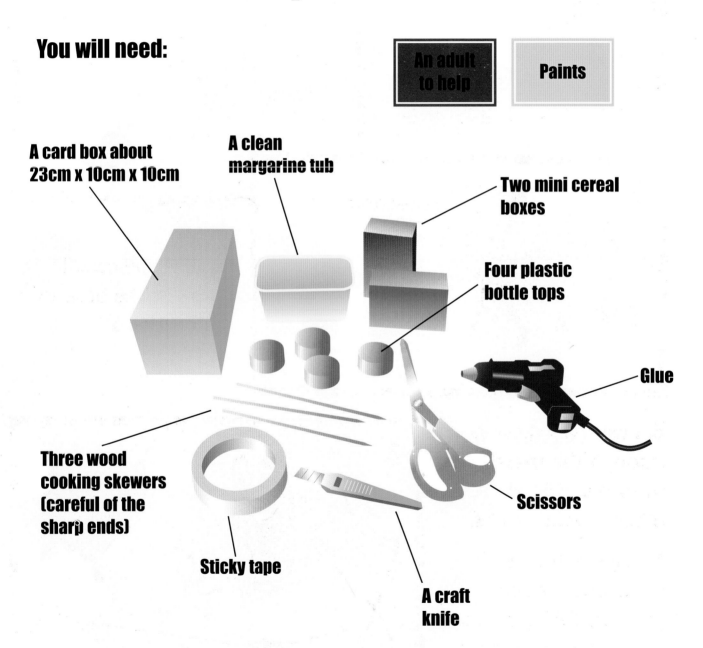

A card box about 23cm x 10cm x 10cm

A clean margarine tub

Two mini cereal boxes

Four plastic bottle tops

Glue

Three wood cooking skewers (careful of the sharp ends)

Sticky tape

A craft knife

Scissors

SAFETY! An adult must help you with the cutting and sticking.

1. Cut out a long side from the large box as shown to make the base of your truck.

1. 2cm rim

2. Cereal boxes

2. Glue the cereal boxes to the base to make the cab.

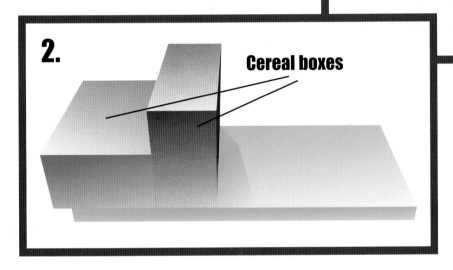

3. Push two skewers through the truck base from one side to the other to make axles.

Make small holes in the centres of the plastic bottle tops. Push them onto the axles to make wheels. Trim the axles to length.

3. Axles

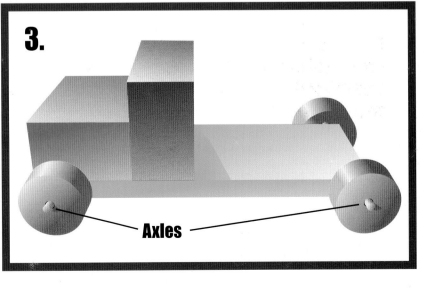

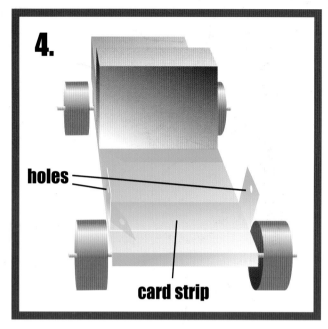

4. holes

card strip

4. Cut a strip of card about 18cm x 3cm from the spare part of the large box.

Bend up both ends to make tabs. Make holes at each end.

Glue the strip near the back of the truck as shown. This is where the margarine tub is fixed to make the dumper body.

5. Make small holes near the base of the tub. Push a skewer through one card tab, the tub and the other tab.

Make sure the tub can tip up and down.

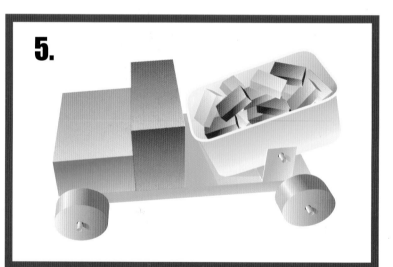

5.

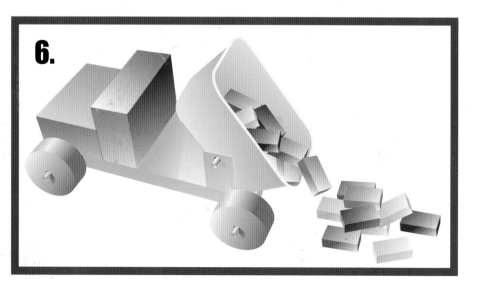

6.

6. Paint your truck.

Use it to carry a load.

Tip the body to dump the load.

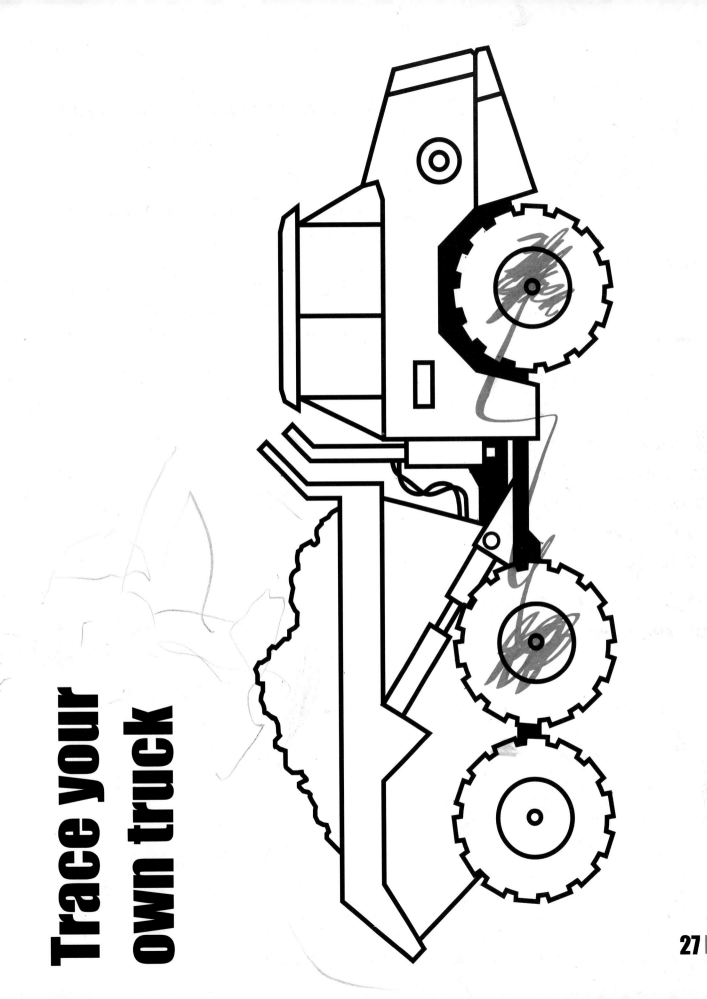

Trace your own truck

Truck words

air horn
A powerful horn worked by air. Truck drivers sound the horn to warn other drivers they are coming.

articulated truck
A truck with a separate tractor unit and trailer. The truck bends between the tractor and trailer as it turns a corner.

axle
The rod through the centre of a wheel.

cab
The part of a truck in which the driver sits.

diesel
The fuel a truck engine uses to make it go.

dumper truck
A tough truck that carries soil and rocks.

engine
The part that makes the power to move a truck.

hydraulic ram

The part on a dumper truck that tips the trailer. The ram is worked by oil, which pushes a rod called a piston along a cylinder.

lorry

Another name for a road truck.

quarry

A place where stone is removed from the ground by digging. Dumper trucks carry the stone.

rigid truck

A truck with the tractor and trailer fixed together. A rigid truck does not bend as it turns corners.

road train

A long truck with two or more trailers.

tractor unit

The front part of the truck with the cab and engine.

trailer

The back part of the truck that carries the load.

Index